"The One Page Business Plan
does something outrageous!
It causes very busy people
to stop and think.
As they start to write...
it confirms both their clarity
and their confusion!"

— Jim Horan
President
The One Page Business Plan Company

WARNING – DISCLAIMER

This book was designed to provide information in regard to the subject matter covered. It is not the purpose of this manual to reprint all of the information available to the author/publisher, but to complement, amplify and supplement other sources.

Use of The One Page Business Plan® does not in any way guarantee the success of an idea or organization, nor does it ensure that financing will be made available. When legal or expert assistance is required, the services of a competent professional should be sought.

The author/publisher shall have neither liability nor responsibility to any person or entity with respect to any loss or damage caused, or alleged to be caused, directly or indirectly by the information contained in this book.

If you do not wish to be bound by the above, you may return this book to the publisher for a full refund.

THE ONE PAGE BUSINESS PLAN - PROFESSIONAL CONSULTANT EDITION

Copyright © 2006 - 2017 The One Page Business Plan Company, All rights reserved.

The One Page and The One Page Business Plan are registered trademarks.

No part of this book may be used or reproduced in any manner whatsoever without written permission except in the case of brief quotations embodied in articles and reviews.

Published by:

The One Page Business Plan Company
1798 Fifth Street
Berkeley, CA 94710
Phone: (510) 705-8400
Fax: (510) 705-8403
www.onepagebusinessplan.com

ISBN-13: 978-1-891315-04-6
ISBN-10:   1-891315-04-8

FIRST EDITION - v.5, Ninth Printing

Book Design by: Melodie Lane
Cover design by: Jim McCraigh
Edited by: Rebecca Salome Shaw
Photography by: Wentling Studio, Inc.

Printed in the United States of America

The One Page Business Plan®

*The Fastest, Easiest Way
to Write a Business Plan!*

By Jim Horan

Professional Consultant Edition

Foreword

What the world's leading author of business best-sellers is saying about The One Page Business Plan®...

"The One Page Business Plan is an out-and-out winner. Period. It makes great sense to me as a so-called business thinker. But the acid test was applying it to a start-up I co-founded. We spent several days drafting our one pager - and have been editing it ever since. It is a powerful, living document; the very nature of which has led us to important new insights.

The One Page Business Plan = the proverbial better mouse trap!"

- Tom Peters
author of
Leadership,
Re-imagine!,
In Search of Excellence,
Thriving on Chaos,
The Pursuit of Wow!,
and The Circle of Innovation

What Others Are Saying

The One Page Business Plan® takes a complex process and makes it simple!

This is a friendly, but no nonsense approach to business planning that got me over my reluctance to write a business plan. This process got me to think out of the box! And to actually get my plan written! One Page Plans rock!
Kendall Moalem, Kendall Moalem Design & Consulting

As a business owner and consultant, I've had a number of business plans, but none of them were effective. Having all the essentials of our plan on one page helped get me and my consulting partners get and stay on track!
Norman Kurtin, Master Instructional Designer, Re: Mind

I had been writing the same goals and visions for my business over and over. What I wrote in March, I wrote in June, and again in September. After I heard Jim speak, I wrote my one page plan. I now choose my opportunities more wisely and waste less time because I have my plan in place.
Linda Pollock, Professional Organizer

The One Page Business Plan truly helps the prospective entrepreneur or existing business owner get focused and clear on one page. When they are clear on one page, they have a much better chance for success! As a consultant, I now have a One Page Plan, and I am much more focused and clear.
Greg Garrett, Consultant & Program Manager, One Stop Capital Shop

It's easy for a stockbroker to get wrapped up in the market and lose perspective that you are in business for yourself. In order to be successful for the long run, one must have a plan and The One Page Business Plan is a great tool.
Ralph Miljanich, Sr. Financial Advisor/Consultant, Vice President, Morgan Stanley, Inc.

The One Page Business Plan is the business plan for independent professionals. It de-mystifies business planning so that the average business professional can actually write a business plan that makes sense!
Rebecca Salome, Entrepreneurial Authors

Jim's presentation on The One Page Business Plan was absolutely enlightening! I finally realized that as a therapist, I am an entrepreneur and a business owner. I now have a business plan that is helping me build my practice.
Mia Salaverry, MFCC

I quickly glanced at The One Page Business Plan format and knew it was what I was looking for. Within a couple of hours, I had my first draft. Now I have a business plan that I really understand.
Norman Meshriy, Career Insights, author of "Outside the Cubicle".

I've written the long business plans more than once and they sat gathering dust. They were too involved to help me stay on track. The One Page Business Plan makes planning doable, flexible, and usable.
Elaine Groen R.D., Nutrition Source

I recommend The One Page Business Plan to anyone wanting to free themselves from the fear and terror of writing a business plan. Jim's book is totally user-friendly, highly efficient, and best of all fun.
Jan St. John, Founder of 21st Century Radio Production

*"You must
simplify.
You must make
the complex simple,
then you must
make it work."*

— I.M. Pei
Master Architect

Author's Note

Most likely you have a one person consulting practice... it is a simple business. This book was created for you!

The problem with most planning processes is that they are too complex... and they take too long! It is highly likely you have attempted many times to create a business plan either from scratch or using planning software... and are now more frustrated than ever because you do not have a simple plan for your consulting practice.

You need a simple structure and process for capturing your thoughts... about your business.   We are going to help you!

The One Page Business Plan® was created in 1994 for people like you. Many of my early clients were proprietors of know-how. They were consultants, coaches, therapists, educators, trainers, attorneys, CPAs, business process experts... etc! They all had lots of great ideas! So many... they were in fact paralyzed. They wanted to get their ideas organized, prioritized and actionable. They knew they could not do everything they wanted to... all at once! They needed a simple plan.

In this book I am not going to preach on the benefits of planning. You already know them... you preach them to your clients. In fact, you probably sell some form of planning services on a regular basis. We are going to help you write a clear, concise plan... simply and easily.

This book has been streamlined for consultants.   It is absolutely the fastest, easiest way to create a plan for a consulting practice. Using the One Page Plan methodology, you do not have to start with a blank page. We have created templates and examples that reflect the latest thinking and practical application of the best practices in the industry. We think we have done a lot of the hard work for you.   We are glad to be with you on this journey.

By the way, yes, I do have a One Page Plan! They say we teach what we need to learn. I have been a full-time student of this process for over 30 years. It continues to confirm what I know and what I don't know about my business.

Jim Horan
Author, Consultant, Speaker

How to Use This Book and eToolkit

The primary purpose of this book is to help you get your plan onto paper. It has been carefully crafted to capture the plan that is in your head.

Carry this book with you, write in it, use it as a container for capturing your thoughts as they occur. If you have multiple businesses, partners or managers, have them get their own copy.

It's not necessary to do all the exercises in this book. If you can write your One Page Business Plan by reviewing the samples — skip the exercises. They are there to help guide you through the process if you need help.

This book does not look like the typical business planning book — it isn't intended to. The exercises and examples are meant to stimulate you. The graphics and images are meant to guide you. If they look playful, be playful and explore. If they look analytical, be analytical and focused. The examples and samples are from real business plans. They are meant to show you how powerful a few words or a well-constructed phrase can be.

Do not underestimate the power of the questions that appear simple! They are simple by design. If you do not get an "aha" from them, have somebody ask you the questions. Important insights may begin to flow.

This book is divided into nine sections with the focus on the five elements of The One Page Business Plan. You can start anywhere. It's OK to jump around!

There are many different ways to use and interact with this book. Exercises can be done:

- by oneself

- with a planning partner (2 or more consultants)

- as a management team

- as a group

- with a paid advisor

 The Consultant's eToolkit (download link on the last page of the book) contains the One Page Business Plan templates, bonus exercises, One Page budget worksheet, plus Scorecards for monitoring and tracking your results.

It also contains several articles on critical sales and marketing best practices you must master in order to build a successful consulting practice!

Business Plan Myths

- All business plans are in writing.

- They must be long to be good.

- Their primary purpose is to obtain financing.

- It's easier for others to write business plans.

- You can and should do it by yourself.

- It takes six months, a significant amount of executive and staff's time, and expensive consultants.

- If completed, it will sit unused on a bookshelf.

- My practice is too small; business plans are for much bigger organizations.

- I know where I am taking my business; I do not need a written business plan.

- I can just pay for a consultant to write the plan for me; that will be good enough.

Let's dispel the myths...

Table of Contents

VISION

MISSION

OBJECTIVES

STRATEGIES

ACTION PLANS

Introduction

What is a One Page Business Plan?

"Planning is a process... not an event!

One Page Plans are living, changing, evolving documents!"

The One Page Business Plan is an innovative approach to business planning that captures the essence of any business, project or program on a single page using key words and short phrases.

Most companies use the process to create not only the company's overall plan, but to create a plan for each supporting department, project and program. Since the creation of The One Page Business Plan in 1994, over 500,000 companies have successfully used the process to bring structure, alignment and accountability to their organizations. Many of those companies were professional services firms.

The flexible methodology makes it possible for entrepreneurs, business owners, executives, managers and professionals in any organization to each have a plan. The standard format makes it easy to review, compare and understand plans.

One Page Business Plans work because:

- Plans actually get documented
- Plans are understandable
- Plans are easy to write, easy to update
- Every manager or team has one

The process creates:

- Alignment
- Accountability
- Results

Our Observations...

Why One Page?

You are busy; your time is limited. You want to spend your time being billable. Creating products and services. Marketing and selling your services. You are action and results oriented. Most of us are not good at prose writing... it takes too long to write a well-written sentence, paragraph, page or chapter. And far too long to read. People need to be able to read a plan in about five minutes. They want the essence... the key points. Then they want to talk... to ask clarifying questions, come to agreement... and then take action.

Why Plan?

Some need to write plans to get funding... however since few consulting practices are fundable other than by friends and family, funding is not the primary reason consultants write plans. Most people write plans because they either want or need to achieve different or better results. Plans are blueprints; they describe what is going to be built, how it will be done, and by whom... and the results to be measured.

Why Written Plans?

The spoken word is too fluid; we have a tendency to ramble. When we speak we almost never say it exactly the same way... frequently we forget to share some of the most important details... or spend too much time on the unimportant things. When we write, we choose our words more carefully. Writing takes time, usually much more than talk. The written word requires a higher level of mindfulness and attention to detail. The written word also produces a contract with yourself and others that can be reread, refined... a source for refection and mindful change if necessary.

Asking people simple questions... works!

People love to talk about their business! They can easily answer questions like, what are you building, what will your practice look like in three years, what has made your consulting business successful to date, what are the critical practice development projects and programs you have underway or planned, what do you measure to know if you are on track... and of course, why does your business exist?

The Power is in 5 Key Questions!

Business plan terminology is problematic. Depending on where you went to school, and the companies/organizations you have worked for... the terms Vision, Mission, Objectives, Strategies and Plans probably mean something different to you than the person sitting next to you. We have learned that business planning "definitions" just don't work. We have refined our questions over twelve years with thousands of business owners. The five questions we will teach you are simple, easy to remember and they will help get your business plan out of your head and onto paper.

About Planning Processes

Starting with a blank page wastes valuable time!

The examples and the fill-in-the-blank prompts are learning aids... designed to help you learn and master the One Page Business Plan technique quickly. We have learned that most people learn by seeing examples, so we give you lots of them.

The dreaded "writer's block" can easily be eliminated by the use of our proprietary fill-in-the-blank templates. They make the creation of any portion of your business plan easy. Use the fill-in-the-blank templates to quickly capture your thoughts and create the first draft. You will also find that the extensive list of templates can spark your thinking and make sure that you are concerned with your "total" business.

Everyone on your team can and should write a One Page Business Plan!

The number one issue business owners and executives share with us is that they need people to work on the right things... and achieve specific results! Partners complain they are not on the same page! There is a simple solution: have your partners, associates, strategic alliance partner, managers and paid staff create One Page Business Plans for their businesses, profit centers, departments, projects or programs. Do not assume they are executing your plan. Have them create their own!

Final Thought: Plans are important... Execution is critical!

Consulting companies invest in planning because they want and need results. Plans are valuable because they provide the blueprint for where you are taking your practice and how you will get there... but ultimately the plans are only as good as the execution. Establish processes such as the scorecard tracking and monthly progress reviews to monitor the implementation of your plans.

Business Plan Terminology is Confusing

There are no universally acceptable definitions to the terms Vision, Mission, Objectives, Strategies or Action Plans. How you use these terms depends entirely on what school you went to and what companies you have worked for. Many companies never successfully complete their business plans because they cannot agree on the basic terminology. We solved the problem!

We translated the five standard business plan elements into five simple and universal questions:

Vision: What are you building?

Mission: Why does this business exist?

Objectives: What results will you measure?

Strategies: How will you build this business?

Action Plans: What is the work to be done?

Writing a business plan for a department or program?

Modify the Mission and Strategy questions by replacing the word "business" with department or program:

Department Usage

Mission: Why does this department exist?

Strategy: How will you build this department?

Program Usage

Mission: Why does this program exist?

Strategy: How will you build this program?

Business Plans Can be Simple and Clean

The best way to understand The One Page Business Plan is to read one... One Page Business Plans can generally be read in about five minutes or less.

The HR Consulting Group

Sally McKenzie & Bob Wilson
FY2018 Consolidated Plan

vision

Within the next 3 years grow The HR Consulting Group into a $1 million North Texas consulting and training company specializing in human resource training and consulting services for companies within a 50 mile radius of Dallas/Ft. Worth that have between 50 and 500 employees.

mission

Bring Preventative HR Programs to Growing Companies!

objectives

- Achieve 2018 sales of $350,000.
- Earn pre-tax profits of $75,000; after paying two partner salaries of $100,000.
- Consistently have partners bill out 6 days per month at $1,500 per day.
- Generate $40,000 from audits & assessments.
- Increase training program & product revenue from $7,500 a month to $10,000 by Aug. 30th.
- Increase avg. bi-weekly attendance at employer council meetings from 12 to 20 by May 15th.
- Produce six notable, publishable case studies this year.
- Take a minimum of 2 one-week vacations in the next twelve months.

strategies

- Become known for preventing catastrophic employee problems that destroy businesses.
- Attract clients with 50 to 500 employees, business owners who want preventive solutions.
- Promote initial trial through our monthly employer council meetings & low-cost guide books.
- Generate revenues thru preventive audits & assessments, training programs & consulting.
- Use technology/Internet for tele-classes, audits & assessments & selling training guides.
- Strategically align our firm w/ local employment law attorneys, CPAs & business consultants.
- Continue to create books, guides, audiotapes & assessment products from existing services.
- Build a business that is ultimately not dependent on our presence; which will make it sellable.

action plans

- Publish "Employer's Bill of Rights Handbook" by Feb. 28th.
- Complete Sexual Harassment, Family Leave & Diversity Guidebooks by April 20th.
- Launch "New Manager Training Series" May 1st; repeat program once in Q3 & Q4.
- Begin hosting monthly "Managers Problem Solving Roundtable" in July.
- Complete makeover of website & e-commerce systems by Sept. 30th.
- Introduce Smart System's web-employee appraisal process to our clients starting Nov. 1st.

Assessment

What's working? What's not?

"Too many people over plan and under execute.

Plan for what is critical... then execute the plan."

Intuitively you know the status of your consulting practice... but when is the last time you stopped and gave it a checkup? Took a real look under the hood?

The 10 Point Assessment on the next two pages is specifically designed for professional advisory practices like yours. These ten assessment areas should help you to quickly take the pulse of your company, which areas are strong, which aspects need attention... and those areas that you just have not gotten to yet.

Here are brief descriptions of the categories:

1.	New Client Acquisition	Outreach, introductions, referrals, on-boarding, engagement initiation
2.	Marketing	Branding, collateral, public relations, Internet
3.	Sales	Pipeline mgt, closing ratio, engagement size/value, add-on sales, repeat business
4.	Strategic Alliances	Referral resources, resource partners, product extension thru certifications, licensing, franchise
5.	Consulting Delivery	Deliverables, client satisfaction, scope mgt, quality, technology, stress level
6.	Public Speaking	Frequency, quality, audience ratings, impact
7.	Productization	Articles, books, software, audio/video products
8.	Professional Development	Research, seminars, advanced degrees
9.	Administrative Functions	Contracts, bookkeeping, taxes, technology
10.	Profitability/Cash Flow	Cash positive, adding to savings, taxes current

The left page is designed to help you quickly assess your total practice. The right page is designed to help you focus in at a more granular level. This entire exercise should take no more than about 15 minutes. Then move on. You can come back and reflect on it later as you are working on other aspects of your One Page Plan.

If you have multiple people in your practice, have everyone do the assessment and then compare and discuss the results.

What's Working in Your Consulting Practice?

Step 1: Rate each of these practice areas on a scale of 1 to 10; 1 = disaster 10 = brilliantly successful.

Step 2: Reflect on why you scored each element the way you did. Circle one or more of the reasons that influenced the rating. (FTI = Failure to Implement, ½♥ = half heartily executed plan, External = external forces, i.e. economy)

	Significance Rating	Rating scale
1. New Client Acquisition		1 2 3 4 5 6 7 8 9 10 FTI ½♥ People Process Time $$ External
2. Marketing		1 2 3 4 5 6 7 8 9 10 FTI ½♥ People Process Time $$ External
3. Sales		1 2 3 4 5 6 7 8 9 10 FTI ½♥ People Process Time $$ External
4. Strategic Alliances		1 2 3 4 5 6 7 8 9 10 FTI ½♥ People Process Time $$ External
5. Consulting Delivery		1 2 3 4 5 6 7 8 9 10 FTI ½♥ People Process Time $$ External
6. Public Speaking		1 2 3 4 5 6 7 8 9 10 FTI ½♥ People Process Time $$ External
7. Productization of Intellectual Property		1 2 3 4 5 6 7 8 9 10 FTI ½♥ People Process Time $$ External
8. Professional Development		1 2 3 4 5 6 7 8 9 10 FTI ½♥ People Process Time $$ External
9. Administrative Functions		1 2 3 4 5 6 7 8 9 10 FTI ½♥ People Process Time $$ External
10. Profitability/Cash Flow		1 2 3 4 5 6 7 8 9 10 FTI ½♥ People Process Time $$ External
Overall Assessment		**1 2 3 4 5 6 7 8 9 10**

Step 3: Make a check mark in the Significance Rating box for 3 to 4 elements you must dramatically improve in the next 6 to 12 months. It is highly doubtful you can make all of them 10s in the next year.

Key Projects... Specific Ideas for Improvement

In left column: Identify key projects or areas that influenced your assessment.
In right column: Quickly brainstorm actions that can be taken to improve execution/performance.

Key Projects	Action to Improve or Maintain

Example for New Client Acquisition:	
New Client Campaign	More phone contact, less emphasis on collateral, more listening, offer better solutions

VISION
MISSION
OBJECTIVES
STRATEGIES
ACTION PLANS

The Vision Statement

What are you building?

"If you don't get the words right... you might build the wrong business!"

Everybody is building something... a company, an organization, or a department. Well-written Vision Statements answer the question: What is being built?... in three sentences or less!

Effective Vision Statements need not be long, but must clearly describe what you are building. A few key words will go a long way. Create a picture of what your company will look like in 1, 3 or even 5 years.

Vision Statements answer these questions:

- What type of company is this?
- What markets does it serve?
- What is the geographic scope?
- Who are the target customers?
- What are the key products and services?
- How big will the company be?
- What will revenues be?
- How many employees will there be?

Almost everyone has a Vision for their company, but some are better at articulating it. Many people struggle with capturing their Vision effectively in writing. At the One Page Business Plan Company we have learned that with a little prompting, most executives, even consultants can capture the essence of their Vision in just a few minutes.

Interview Exercise

Slightly overwhelmed? Want to make the process inclusive? Invite a trusted advisor to interview you using the questions below. Have them interview you in person or over the phone. Have them ask you the questions and record your responses. You might consider doing this interview process with more than one person.

1. Who's the perfect client?

Describe three characteristics of the ideal recipient of your service/product:

Describe three characteristics of clients you would be better off NOT SERVING:

2. What's the service or product?

Describe three characteristics of your service or product:

Describe three things your service or product WON'T DO:

3. What's the competitive environment?

Describe three characteristics of successful consulting practices you admire and WOULD like to emulate:

Describe three characteristics of consultants you WILL NOT emulate:

Crafting Your Vision Statement

Getting the first draft onto paper is always the most difficult. It is infinitely easier to edit! The fill-in-the-blank-template below is geared to help you quickly create a first draft. Each blank in essence is a question; complete all the blanks, and you create a first draft... quickly and easily! Not able to fill in all of the blanks at this time? Don't worry... complete those that you can! Revisit the blanks later, you may need to do some research or enlist help from others.

Vision Statement

Within the next _____ years grow _____ into a $_____
                                    (company name)   (est. annual sales)

_____   _____ company providing
(geographic scope)   (type of business)
(local/region/nat'l/int'l)

_____
                        (list 2-3 of your key products/services)

to _____.
                        (list 2-3 key clients/customers)

The following Vision Statement was created using the fill-in-the-blanks template and then edited. It is brief, but very clear.

"Within the next <u>3 years</u> grow <u>CFO Consulting Services</u> into a <u>$250,000</u> <u>San Francisco Bay Area</u> <u>financial management company</u> specializing in <u>strategic planning, budgeting, forecasting and other financial management best practices</u> for <u>companies that are large enough to have a Controller</u>, but not large enough to have a full time Chief Financial Officer."

Mission

Why does this consulting practice exist?

Mission Statements always answer the question, "Who will we serve and what will we do for them?"

Every company exists for a reason. Good Mission Statements describe why your product, service, department, project, program or business exists. Great Mission Statements are short and memorable. They communicate in just a few words (6 to 8 words are ideal) the company's focus and what is being provided to customers. They always answer the question, "Why will customers buy this product or service?"

Some of the best Mission Statements are an integral part of a company's branding strategy that compels customers to buy, but the same Mission Statements can and do direct and influence all significant management decisions.

Mission Statements answer these specific questions:

- Why does this business exist?
- What is our unique selling proposition?
- What are we committed to providing to our customers?
- What promise are we making to our clients?
- What wants, needs, desires, pain or problems do our products/services solve?

Crafting Your Mission Statement

Experiment with 6 to 8 key words (max. 12 words) that describe why your company exists from your customer's point of view. Capture your competitive marketing edge or unique selling proposition.

Why does this consulting practice exist?

1st Attempt:

We help _____ _____!
   (recipient of your services)   (goal or benefit of your services)

2nd Attempt:

3rd Attempt:

Examples of Mission Statements

The best Mission Statements are short and memorable! And eight words or less!

They may also evoke an emotional response through humor or the senses. Well-written Mission Statements attract customers and also drive behavior within an organization.

As you review these Company Mission Statements, ask yourself how well they answer the question, "Why does this company exist?"

ELA Consulting Group	We make companies smarter about their business!
Consulting CFOs	We are the small business financial navigators!
Entrepreneurial Authors	Every professional has a book in them... we help get it out!
Pratt Ranch Management	Healthy Land, Happy Families, Profitable Businesses... Ranching for Profit.
Nurseprenuer	We provide health care professionals training that prevents injuries and saves lives.
Beauty Resource	We're the Salon and Spa Business Experts!
ProAttitude	We end stress through a fundamental shift in attitude that restores the potential to be great!
Business Growth Strategies	We create break-through market plans!
Career Insights	We help people in career transition think "Outside the Cubicle".

VISION
MISSION
OBJECTIVES
STRATEGIES
ACTION PLANS

Objectives
What will be measured?

Objectives are short statements that quantify the end results of any work effort. Good Objectives are easy to write and are instantly recognizable. They answer the question "What will we measure?"

Objectives clarify what you are trying to accomplish in specific, measurable terms. For an Objective to be effective, it needs to be a well-defined target with quantifiable elements. It is important to include different types of Objectives that cover the entire scope of your professional practice.

Well conceived Objectives:

- Provide a quantitative pulse of the business
- Focus resources towards specific results
- Define success in a measurable manner
- Give people/organizations specific targets
- Establish a framework for accountability and incentive pay
- Minimize subjectivity and emotionalism
- Measure the end results of work effort

Although there is no magical number of Objectives, a One Page Business Plan can accommodate nine. Consider two to three Objectives for sales or revenue, one for profitability, two or three for marketing, one or two that are process oriented.

Objectives Must be Graphable

The One Page methodology makes writing Objectives simple... All Objectives must be graphable!

Everyone learns early in their career that what you measure is what gets improved. If you are serious about growing a profitable consulting practice that is cash flow positive... chart your critical success factors. Have a chart for billable days or hours, total revenues, number of speaking engagements... whatever you know is critical for your success.

Charts are great... everybody can read charts. It's obvious when you are ahead of goal or not!

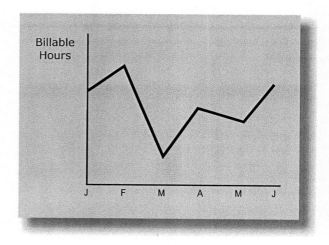

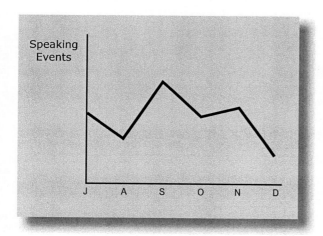

The key to setting meaningful Objectives is to identify goals that are:

- critical to your success and
- can be easily tracked
(*Easily tracked = data is readily available & the specific target can be counted*)

Stated very simply, if you can not count it over time (easily)... it's not an Objective. On the Crafting Objectives exercise, we provide you with a number of frequently used goals in consulting firms... please note, all of them are graphable!

It's easy to craft meaningful Objectives when you use these 3 simple guidelines:

- Write only Objectives that can be graphed
- Include a numerical value in every Objective
- Assign a name & date to assure accountability

A Simple Formula for Writing Objectives...

> *Action To Be Taken*
> +
> *Something Countable*
> +
> *Target/Completion Date*

Here are some examples using this formula:

- Increase consulting revenues from $95,000 in 2013 to $150,000 in 2018.

- Achieve profit before tax of $125,000.

- Sell 100 billable hours every month beginning June 1st.

- Add 10 new clients in 2018; 4 in 1st half, 2 in Q3 & 4 in Q4.

- Increase average consulting engagement from $15,000 to $25,000.

- Give at least 8 presentations in 1st half 2018; 12 in 2nd half.

- Commit to writing 2 articles per quarter in 2018.

- Increase proprietary product sales from $30,000 to $70,000.

- Increase total hours per month of community service from 4 to 6 effective March 1st.

- Take a minimum of three weeks vacation in 2018.

- Increase number of free days per month from 1 to 3.

Crafting Your Objectives

Listed below are templates for Objectives that are fairly common for consulting firms. They are designed to help you quickly create a first draft. It is possible, but not likely all of these templates will work for your firm. If you do not see a template for an Objective that you need, create your own using the others as a model.

Sales	Achieve 2018 sales of $ _____ .
Profit	Earn pre-tax profit in 2018 of $ _____ .
# of Clients	Increase number of active clients from _____ to _____ .
Average Engagement	Increase average engagement from $_____ to $_____ .
Project Sales	Sell _____ projects or engagements at $_____ for a total of $_____ .
Billable Hours	Increase average monthly billable hours from _____ to _____ .
Public Speaking	Give at least _____ presentations in 1st half 2018; _____ in 2nd half.
Publishing	Commit to writing _____ articles per quarter in 2018. Total articles_____ .
Product Sales	Increase _____ product sales from $_____ to $ _____ .
Community Service	Increase (decrease) total hours of community service from _____ to _____ .
Free Time	Commit to _____ weeks of vacation in 2018 and _____ free days.

Remember, your One Page Plan can accommodate up to nine Objectives.

Sample Objectives...

Here are three sets of Objectives from three very different companies. In these examples there are 6 to 8 Objectives that describe "what these professional service firms will measure each month over the next 12 months to determine if they are on track." Some of these Objectives are rather traditional, others are a little unique. Hopefully they will get you to think creatively about your business... and what counts!

The Emergency IT Doctors

- Achieve 2018 sales of $500,000.
- Earn pre-tax profit of $60,000 after paying expenses and 3 principal salaries of $100,000.
- Increase number of active clients from 100 to 150 by June 30th.
- Reduce average client downtime from 6 hours to 4 hours.
- Reduce crisis response time from 2 hours to 1 hour.
- Increase percent of clients on remote technical service support program from 38% to 65%.
- Secure 150 PC audits in first six months of year to assure 33% conversion ratio.
- Reduce average OT from 26% to 10% by supplementing permanent staff w/ qualified temps.

Wealth Builders

- Increase assets under management from $15 to $25 million.
- Increase income after business expenses from $150,000 to $220,000 in 2018.
- Increase ROA from .85% to 1.0%
- Increase average acct. from $250,000 to $600,000 in three years; $350,000 by Dec. 2018.
- Increase number of active accounts from 60 to 72 by year end.
- Volunteer 10 hours a month with the American Red Cross.
- Take a total of 30 days of vacation and free days in 2018.

Leaders by Design

- Achieve 2018 consulting revenues of $175,000.
- Earn pre-tax profit of $105,000.
- Increase number of active clients from 4 to 6 by July 1st.
- Speak at least once a month in 1st half of year, 10 times in 2nd half; total speaking gigs 16.
- Produce one Leadership by Design executive retreat per quarter; yielding $15,000 each.
- Create & publish one 600 to 800 word article per month; be positioned to write book in 2019.
- Reduce personal time on administrivia to less than 6 hours per week.
- Decrease my weight from 210 to 180 pounds by year end.

VISION
MISSION
OBJECTIVES
STRATEGIES
ACTION PLANS

Strategies

How will this business be built?

Success is rarely an accident. It is usually the result of executing a carefully crafted set of strategies. Strategies provide a blueprint or road map for building and managing the company. They also provide a comprehensive overview of the company's business model and frequently say as much about what the company will not do, as what it will do.

Strategies set the direction, philosophy, values, and methodology for building and managing your company. They establish guidelines and boundaries for evaluating business decisions. Following a predefined set of strategies is critical to keeping a business on track.

One way of understanding strategies is to think of them as industry practices. Every industry has its leaders, its followers and its rebels, and each has an approach for capturing market share. Pay attention to the successful businesses in your industry and you can learn important lessons. You can also learn a lot from the failures in your industry.

Strategies are not secret. In fact they are common knowledge and openly shared in every industry. Pick up any industry's publication and you will know precisely what the industry's leaders have to say about the opportunities and how to capitalize on them. These leaders will also share their current problems and their solutions. This is critical information for building and managing your business. Capture the best thinking/best practices from your industry along with the strategies that make your company distinct and you will have a powerful set of strategies that drive your company forward!

In summary, Strategies are broad statements, covering multiple years that:

- Set the direction, philosophy, values
- Define the business model
- Establish guidelines for evaluating important decisions
- Set limits on what a company will do or will not do

There are many moving parts to a successful consulting practice. There are a lot of decisions to be made. Many of the decisions are personal preference.

Keep in mind that nobody gets all the parts and pieces in place before they start... it takes time; probably three to five years. Review this list; use it as a catalyst to think about what will actually be necessary to make your consulting practice successful over time. As you are crafting your Strategies on page 40, refer back to this page.

☐ Personal Expertise	☐ Value Proposition	☐ Trademarks/Patents
☐ Business Success	☐ Price Point: Hi, Mid, Low	☐ Geographical Area Served
☐ Technical Knowledge	☐ Importance of Quality	☐ Customer Service
☐ Reputation	☐ Availability & Access	☐ Board of Advisors
☐ Referral Sources	☐ Productizing Your Services	☐ Use of Technology
☐ Partners or Going Solo	☐ Publishing: Self or Trade	☐ Employees
☐ Strategic Alliances	☐ Speaking: Free or Paid	☐ Home Office or Downtown
☐ Company Image	☐ Hi or Low Tech Products	☐ Part or Full Time
☐ Market Presence	☐ Build or Buy Products	☐ Self-funding
☐ Uniqueness of Offering	☐ Licensing & Franchising	☐ Loans or Capital
☐ Product Name	☐ Sell Only Your Services	☐ Amount of Travel
☐ Branding	☐ Sell Other People's Time	☐ Family Support
☐ Ideal Customers	☐ Sell Other People's Skills	☐ Peace of Mind
☐ No. of Clients	☐ Shared Support Services	☐ Amount of Free Time

Deciding Which Strategies Are Appropriate for Your Business

Finding appropriate strategies for your business is not difficult. As you can see from the list above... there are many choices.

Much information is readily available to you for free or at minimal cost. There are probably multiple professional trade associations that serve your niche. Go online and explore. Ask other consultants in your niche where to go to research the latest trends in your industry.

The key question is: which strategies will you select... and at what time in the life cycle of your company? You cannot execute all of your strategies at the same time.

In the early stages of your practice, it is critical that you employ strategies that leverage your expertise, career successes, and your extensive network. Yes, your network is extensive; you may need to rediscover it.

In the early stages pro bono work can be invaluable to help people understand that you are now available in a new capacity.

The most important strategy might be for you to become know as a source of referrals. Want referrals? Give them freely, regularly!

Research Exercise

Review the last three issues of your industry's trade, professional or association journals and answer the questions below.

What and where are the opportunities?	How can you capitalize on them?
What threats exist?	**How can you minimize the threats and/or turn them into opportunities?**

Examples of Issues Affecting Consulting & Professional Service Firms

- Shortage of qualified people
- Client companies demanding more, but may have smaller budgets.
- Consultants are getting older, not willing to work as long as they used to.
- Experienced consultants less willing to have all of their eggs tied up with one or two clients.

- Hourly & daily rate resistance
- Travel has become a major hassle. Consultants less willing to jump on an airplane.
- Use of executive/professional coaches becoming accepted.

A Simple Formula for Writing Strategies...

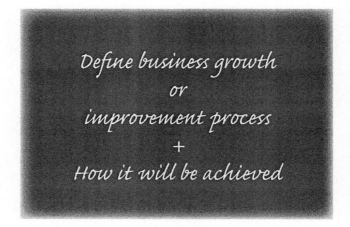

Define business growth
or
improvement process
+
How it will be achieved

Here are some examples using this formula:

Positioning	Become nationally known for solving leadership issues in hospitals.
Perfect Client	Attract/solicit clients that need to master Internet marketing.
Opportunities	Focus on trend to hire baby boomers as supplemental workforce.
Products/ Services	Core services are market research, focus groups & analytical consumer studies.
Initial Trial	Promote initial trial w/ public speaking, free assessments & limited scope projects.
Revenue Model	Generate revenues by sale of services, product sales, public speaking.
Pricing	Price our services at slight premium to market, justified by national recognition.
Consulting Delivery	Primary consulting will be done by me; supplement w/core team of trusted experts.
Technology/ Internet	Use technology/Internet for building awareness/credibility, productization of services.
Strategic Alliances	Use strategic alliances to co-brand, co-market, co-sell & productization.
Productization	Create books, audio tapes & software based on the Always Get the Sale™ process.
Administration	Minimize personal time on admin functions; use part time asst.; invest in software.

We call this exercise, Bend the Curve.

Step 1: Draft a Revenue Objective for your consulting practice for the next 1, 3 or 5 years.

Step 2: Brainstorm up to four Strategies that are necessary to achieve the Objective in Step 1.

Step 3: Identify 2 to 4 key Action Plans per Strategy. Action Plans are typically Projects or Programs.

Increase _____ from _____ to _____ by _____.

(Example: Increase total revenues from $75,000 to $100,000 by 12/31/2018.)

Strategy

Strategy

Strategy

Strategy

<u>Action Plans</u>

_____   _____   _____   _____

_____   _____   _____   _____

_____   _____   _____   _____

_____   _____   _____   _____

Crafting Your Strategies

Listed below is a set of Strategy templates that are common for consulting firms. The templates are designed to help you quickly create a first draft. It is unlikely your firm will need all of these Strategies, but this set of templates should help you focus on how you will build your consulting practice... and what will make it successful over time.

Positioning	Become nationally known for solving _____ & _____ problems.
Perfect Client	Attract/solicit clients that need _____, _____ & _____.
Opportunities	Focus on _____, _____ & _____ trends/opportunities.
Products/Services	Core products/services are _____, _____ & _____.
Revenue Model	Generate revenues by _____, _____ & _____.
Pricing	Our pricing strategy is _____, _____ & _____.
Initial Trial	Promote initial trial by _____, _____ & _____.
Consulting Delivery	Consulting will be delivered by _____, _____ & _____.
Technology/Internet	Use technology/Internet for _____, _____ & _____.
Strategic Alliances	Use strategic alliances to _____, _____ & _____.
Productization	Create _____, _____ & _____ products from _____ services.

Remember, your One Page Plan can accommodate up to nine Strategies.

Sample Strategies...

Here are three sets of strategies, from three very different companies. In these examples there are 6 to 8 strategies that describe the "essence of what will make these companies successful over time." These strategies describe business models, best practices, culture and personal preferences. All were initially created with the fill-in-the-blank templates and then edited. Note that each strategy fits on a single line.

The HR Consulting Group

- Become known for preventing catastrophic employee problems that destroy businesses.
- Attract clients with 50 to 500 employees, business owners who want preventive solutions.
- Promote initial trial through monthly employer council meetings & low-cost guide books.
- Generate revenues thru preventive audits & assessments, training programs & consulting.
- Use technology/Internet for tele-classes, audits & assessments & selling training guides.
- Strategically align our firm w/ local employment law attorneys, CPAs & business consultants.
- Continue to create books, guides, audiotapes & assessment products from existing services.
- Build a business that is ultimately not dependent on my presence; making it sellable.

Consulting CFOs

- Focus on companies w/ sales of $3 to $30 million not large enough to have a FT CFO.
- Core advisory services: planning, budgeting, forecasting, cash mgt, financing, risk mgmt.
- Promote initial trial by public speaking, low-cost financial capabilities assessment & seminars.
- Generate revenues thru consulting, CFO & Controller searches, seminars & product commissions.
- Price offerings to yield high margins by bundling services w/ high-value web tools/software.
- Consulting delivered by senior partners, analysis by senior accountants; selectively outsource.
- Use web-based budgeting, planning software apps. that minimize need for client site visits.
- Get referrals by generously giving tax work to CPAs & legal issues to attorneys.

Main Street Business Strategy Group

- Become nat'ly known for renovating 1960s strip malls into vibrant, profitable retail destinations.
- Focus on nat'l trend to revitalize the downtown retail experience.
- Partner w/ real estate developers, boutique & nat'l brand retailers, city redevelopment agencies.
- Primarily generate revenues thru consulting services: research, design, plans and advocacy.
- Use technology/Internet to facilitate research, focus groups, community involvement & advocacy.
- Build nat'l brand & corporate identity by creatively showcasing success stories on national media.

Sage Advice from Successful Consultants...

Consultants talk too much... especially during the sales process. Frequently after listening to a prospect for just a few minutes, they think they have more than enough information to propose one or more solutions. I suggest at the point a consultant thinks they know enough to propose a solution... they take a deep breath, and ask another question! And a few minutes later, when once again they think they have enough information to propose a solution... STOP, take another deep breath... and ask another question. After a consultant has repeated this process three, four or five times... they might know enough to propose a solution. But not necessarily!

Harvey Meier, Harvey A. Meier Co., Inc., Spokane, Washington

Many consultants are uncomfortable discussing pricing and the terms of their consulting engagement face to face. We all too often allow our fear and assumptions sabotage us. I suggest when it's time to talk price, a consultant should take a deep breath, maybe two -- look 'em in the eye, and state their price... without apology.

Toni Nell, Springboard Consulting, Santa Cruz, California

Consultants typically think the sales process is over once they have the CEO's buy-in. In fact, the sale to the CEO, business owner or executive is just the first sale. Regardless of the nature of the consulting engagement, the consultant will almost always have to resell the project to each and every person involved with the project to assure that they will fully participate. The key to successful projects is to have all of the participants understand how their involvement in the project will personally benefit them.

Chuck Fry, Fry Consulting Group, Alameda, California

Most consultants' approach to networking is horrible! They go from one leads group or professional organization to another hoping, sometimes pressuring people into giving them introductions and referrals. And then they wonder why they never get referrals. My suggestion is simple: Get involved with the professional and business groups that make sense for your company. Show up regularly and do everything you can possibly do to help the people in that organization grow their business. Your generosity will come back to you, and your business will grow too! And don't forget: the easiest way to get referrals is to give them.

Jeff Rubin, The Newsletter Guy, Pinole, California

Sometimes, in an earnest quest to offer a solution to our client's need we inadvertently try to close a sale prematurely. What I notice and feel is an instant awkwardness. Other times I may begin to experience that sinking feeling we call rejection. What I have come to learn in either case is my focus has shifted from the client... to me! I am beginning to feel sorry or bad about a pending loss of something I do not even own. That moment of awkwardness is the place where the "business transaction" has overtaken "relationship building". The solution is actually very easy: ask another question! Questions, when from real curiosity, will always shift the focus from you back to the client... where it should be!

Brenda Chaddock, Limitless Leadership, Vancouver, British Columbia

and Corporate Buyers of Consulting Services

An internal consultant with a Fortune 500 company who has purchased millions of dollars of training and consulting over the last 25+ years shared these observations about consultants and their behavior during the bidding and proposal stage of a multi-million dollar consulting engagement.

1. First consultants eliminated were ME CENTERED... they dominated the conversation, told all about their processes, products, past clients. It was all about them. They asked few questions.

2. Second set of consultants eliminated were CONTENT or FACT CENTERED... they knew everything about everything. They quoted all of the latest management books, they were able to quote facts from all of the top surveys and analyses. They had a quote, a fact and the references to back up everything they said. They were undoubtedly very knowledgeable... but without a doubt, they were not going to work with this client.

3. Third set of consulting firms eliminated were PRODUCT CENTERED... these firms offered their product solutions long before they understood the underlying problems. These firms were outstanding at demo-ing their products and espousing the features of the products... .but nobody cared. These firms took no time to understand the real underlying issues.

4. The final two firms were CLIENT ORIENTED... they took time to fully interview the prospective client and understand the underlying issues. They asked tons of questions... finally the interviewing team asked the consultants if they thought they had a solution to the problem. I believe they then asked another question (just joking).

Take time to get to know your prospects... and, "just about the time you think you are ready to offer a solution, ask another question!"

VISION
MISSION
OBJECTIVES
STRATEGIES
ACTION PLANS

Action Plans

Defining the Work to be Done

"Business building projects always compete with marketing and revenue production.

Commit to 1 to 2 major projects per year! They will serve you well!"

Action Plans define the actual work to be done... the specific actions the business must take to implement Strategies and to achieve the Objectives.

For your consulting practice, Action Plans will be major business-building or infrastructure projects. They will undoubtedly focus on the execution of your Marketing, Technology and Productization projects. These projects may require significant capital and expense budgets; for sure they will consume your valuable time, and may take multiple months to complete.

In well-written One Page Business Plans, Action Plans are NEVER "job description tasks".

Ideally, each Action Plan statement relates to an Objective or a Strategy... but it is not necessary to write an Action Plan for every Objective or Strategy in your One Page Business Plan. You will not have enough space... and more importantly you will not have enough time or money to execute all of the projects you can dream up. Your One Page Plan will accommodate up to nine major plans. We suggest you craft no more than two plans per quarter. For small consulting companies... one major project, like writing a book... may be all that is reasonable to accomplish in one year.

Remember: Your One Page Business Plan is designed to capture the most important elements of your plan... not all of the elements. If you find that nine Action Plans are not enough, it's possible you may need to write a separate One Page Plan for one or more of the larger projects... or more likely, you have defined too many projects for this year.

"Work" may be defined three ways:

- Major business-building projects
- Significant infrastructure projects
- Programs/Projects that bend the curves and/or trend lines

A Simple Formula for Writing Action Plans...

Description of Work + Completion Date

Here are some examples using the formula:

- Complete the "Selling Made Easy" book by March 31, 2018; 1st print run by May 31st.
- Launch 2nd quarter Executive Briefing Series w/ "Stress-Free Management" on April 15th.
- Complete re-design of website with e-commerce capabilities by July 31st.
- Build prototype web application to simplify employee appraisal by Oct. 31st.
- Hire part-time administrative assistant by February 28th; Bookkeeper by April 30th.

Work "Bends" the Curve... Project Prioritization

In the Strategy section we used the "Bend the Curve" visual to identify the major opportunities that have the potential to significantly grow your business over the next 3 to 5 years. We can again use this visual model to help identify and prioritize the major projects and programs you and your team are going to focus on in the next twelve months.

When you have agreed on the projects that will bend the curve, assign completion dates and responsibility... then craft the Action Plans. Each of these projects is a potential candidate for your One Page Business Plan! Also be sure to calculate the expense and capital budgets for these projects and get them into your One Page Budget Worksheet, which is included in the Consultant's eToolkit.

Bend the Curve
Projects that Produce Results

Identify 2 to 4 projects or programs you are going to implement this year that have the greatest potential for Bending the Curve(s) in your consulting practice. You might have a Bend the Curve worksheet for Sales, Profitability, Market Awareness and Productivity! Or you might just have one for the entire company. Remember: keep it simple. If a little is good, more does not necessarily make it better.

Increase _____ from _____ to _____ by _____.

(Example: Increase profit before tax from $75,000 to $130,000 in 2018.)

Project D

Project C

Project B

Project A

Resources Required: People, Expense Budget, Capital Budget

_____   _____   _____   _____

_____   _____   _____   _____

_____   _____   _____   _____

The One Page Planning Wheel

The One Page Planning Wheel is another visual tool that helps entrepreneurs, business owners and executives visualize key projects over the entire year.

Most people have little problem identifying critical tasks and near-term projects that need to be completed in the next six days... or six weeks. But the identification, prioritization and calendaring of significant projects and programs in the second half of the year... or beyond, can be difficult when the focus is so often on short term results.

Use The One Page Planning Wheel as a tool to brainstorm the key projects in your company, division, department or program. In the brainstorming phase, identify all major projects, then refine the list down to two or three projects per quarter.

Remember, your One Page Business Plan can accommodate up to nine Action Plans.

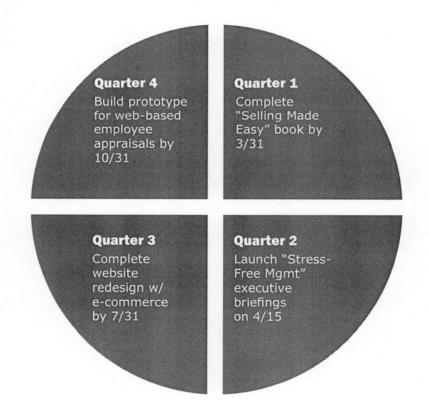

Quarter 4
Build prototype for web-based employee appraisals by 10/31

Quarter 1
Complete "Selling Made Easy" book by 3/31

Quarter 3
Complete website redesign w/ e-commerce by 7/31

Quarter 2
Launch "Stress-Free Mgmt" executive briefings on 4/15

Crafting Your Action Plans

There are four quarters in a year. List one or two major business-building projects that must be accomplished in each of the next four quarters in order to implement your strategies and achieve your overall goals. When complete, type your Action Plans into The One Page Business Plan template that is in the Consultant's eToolkit.

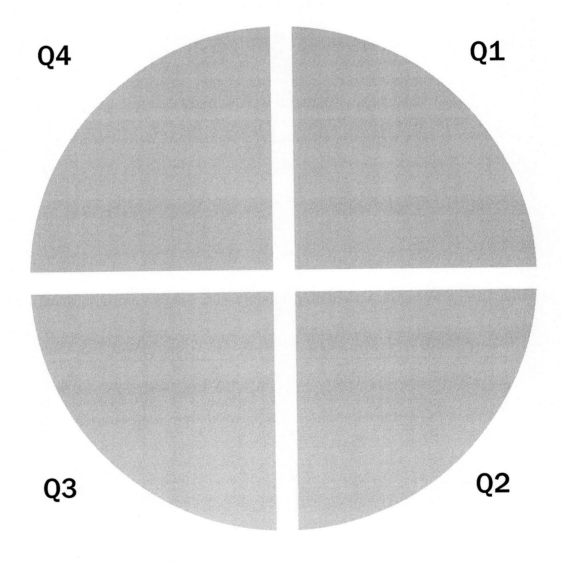

Remember: Time exists so that you do not have to do everything at once.

VISION

MISSION

OBJECTIVES

STRATEGIES

ACTION PLANS

Assembling and Polishing the Plan

"Congratulations!
Your Plan is Now
in Writing...
What's Next?"

Assemble Your Plan onto One Page!

Select one of The One Page Business Plan templates from the Consultant's eToolkit and type in each of the five elements of the plan you created using the various exercises. See last page for eToolkit link.

Step Back and Review Your Plan

How does it look to you? If you are like most people, some parts of your plan will be complete, while other parts will still need editing and additional detail. Don't rush the process! Make the obvious changes now, but allow some time to reflect on your plan.

Carry the plan with you; it's only one page! As new ideas and insights appear, capture them on paper. Review the Polishing and Edit suggestions on the next page. Most people find it takes about three drafts to get their plans in solid shape... don't cut the process short. Too much depends on it.

Review Your Plan with Others

You have a plan... now review it with your partners, team, and/or trusted advisors. Have them ask you clarifying questions. Take good notes on the feedback; you might consider recording the feedback sessions. Update your plan with the feedback you decide is appropriate.

Have Partners? Employees? Have them Create their One Page Business Plan

Executives, managers, teams and partners are expensive! After you have reviewed your plan with your team, and they have had a chance to ask clarifying questions, give them 3 to 7 business days to create their One Page Business Plan. Encourage them to work together; the plans will be more cohesive as a result.

Balance and Align the Plans

Balancing the plans is a process that ensures all of the functions within your company will be working together, on the right projects and programs, in the proper sequence, at the right time... and not at cross purposes.

When your organization's plans are balanced and aligned... you can have everyone, literally, working on the same page!

Editing and Polishing the Plan

Here is a list of ideas and tips to polish your plan:

Overall Review

- Does your Vision Statement describe what you are building?
- Will your Mission Statement attract new clients? Drive employee behavior? Is it memorable?
- Are your Objectives measurable, dated and graphable?
- Do your Strategies describe what will make your business successful over time?
- Are your Action Plans significant business-building projects? Will they achieve your Objectives?

Order and Abbreviation

- Edit Objectives, Strategies, and Action Plan statements to one line.
- Eliminate all unnecessary words and phrases.
- Abbreviate words when necessary.
- Use symbols like "&" in lieu of "and" to save space.
- Use "k" or "m" for thousands and "M" for millions.
- Communicate priority of Objectives, Strategies, and Action Plans by placing them in the proper order.

Creative Considerations

- Use bullets to make key points stand out.
- Highlight key phrases in italics.

Strengthening Exercises

- Edit Vision, Mission and Strategy until they are enduring statements that "resonate!"
- Drop low-priority items. Remember, "less can produce more."
- Refine Objectives and Action Plans to be specific, measurable, and define accountability.

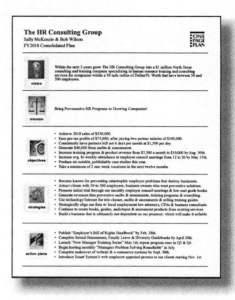

Involve Others

- Few people can write a solid plan by themselves; ask others for feedback.
- Ask your reviewers:
    - Is this plan really strategic? Too optimistic? Too pessimistic?
    - Does it include all of the critical initiatives you have been talking about?
    - Is it too risky? Too safe?
    - Does it reflect your best thinking?
    - What have I overlooked? What do you see that I missed?
- Listen to the feedback, take notes, and ask clarifying questions.
- Revise and update plan for feedback.
- Ask for another round of feedback.
- Most people find it takes at least three drafts to have a solid plan.
- Repeat until you and your reviewers agree it is solid.

Resources, Timelines and Budgets

Having a plan is critical to your success. Here are a few thoughts on other important processes that will help assure your success.

Define the Required Resources

Every project, program and initiative in your plan will need resources... or it will not happen. For each project identify the people, expense, capital budgets and any other resources required to fully execute the plan. The process of identifying the resources may cause you to realize you may not have the capability or capacity of implementing the plan you just wrote. If that is the case, go back and revise the plan.

Project Timelines

Re-review your project start and completion dates. Are they realistic? One of the major problems with all planning processes is the tendency to think we can do more than we actually can. When we complete a major project or initiative... we feel smart! When we have a list of projects that we have not started or are half done... we feel defeated. Take another hard look at your projects for this next year... would you be extraordinarily pleased if you completed just one or two of them? If so, adjust your plan.

Alignment with Partners & Team

If you have partners or a team, it is not unusual to find during the alignment process that the business units within your company contributing to projects and programs will not have consistent and appropriate start and completion times. For each major project or program, create an overall timeline to assure all of the sub-tasks are in alignment with the overall milestones. If project dates get changed... be sure to update the plans accordingly.

Create a Budget

Almost every activity in a business has a stream of revenue or expenses associated with it. Use your One Page Business Plan(s) to help identify all of the sources of revenue, expense and capital. If you need help in budgeting, get it. This is an important part of your success. Included in the Consultant's eToolkit is a simple One Page Budget Worksheet that should be helpful. See link at the back of the book

Recommendation: If a business unit is big enough for a One Page Business Plan, it should have a separate budget.

Implementation... Tracking & Measuring the Plan

Implement Your Plan

Many plans fail because they never get implemented! When great ideas sit on the shelf... nothing happens. Put your plan to work. You can bet your competitors are working on theirs!

Monitor & Measure

Create a Performance Scorecard for each Objective. Remember: Objectives must have a numeric value that is graphable. Included in the Consultant's eToolkit is a fun and easy template for creating Scorecards. You can graph your results against the Budget or Goal, Last Year and Forecast (if appropriate)... you will have a visual picture of all the key metrics in your company. It is very simple and easy to determine if your are ahead of target... or behind.

Monthly Business Review

Recent surveys indicate only 1 in 5 businesses have a regularly scheduled monthly business review meeting to monitor the implementation and execution of their plans.

The monthly business review is a fabulous opportunity to learn what really happened in your business each month. Do a quick review of each of the major projects... are they on track? If not, address the issues and define solutions to get them back on track.

Have a business coach, professional advisor, mentor? Make it a practice to schedule an hour with them each month to review your progress against your plan.

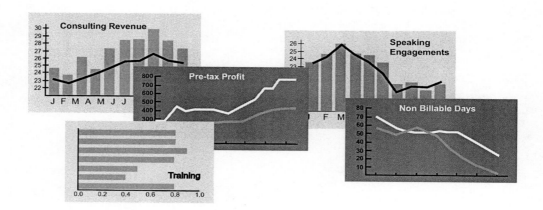

Filling in the Gaps

The process of writing a business plan, in some ways, is like writing a term paper on your business. You capture in writing what you know, conduct research to fill in the gaps, interview knowledgeable people, draft your document, ask for feedback, and then complete the final editing.

Your knowledge of your business is significant. Capture your initial thoughts in the first draft, and then begin the process of reflecting on your plan... and involving others. Keep in mind, the process of planning is one of continual reflection and refinement... and in many ways this is more important than the final document.

Most people have more resources instantly available to them than they realize. These resources are very knowledgeable... and frequently free! They know you, your business, the industry, may share the same clients and may buy from the same vendors.

Resources readily available to you include your team, peer managers, senior executives, Board of Directors, Board of Advisors, vendors, bankers, attorneys, CPAs, and other consultants.

Other significant resources are the national trade associations. They exist to gather and disseminate information about your industry. They follow all of the trends, innovations, opportunities, regulations, etc. Check out their websites, better yet pick up the phone and talk with one of the executives. Get to know the regular contributors.

One of the benefits of The One Page Business Plan is that it can be read in less than five minutes. Share your plan with your resources. Invite their insights and feedback. Your plan will be stronger!

"Your Plan is not finished until it represents your best thinking!"

Sample Plans...

For some, the easiest way to learn how to write a plan is to take a look at how others have written their plans. In this section we have provided four consulting company plans for your review and another nine plans that show the breadth and flexibility of The One Page Business Plan methodology.

There are sample plans for:

- Consulting firms
  - Human Resources
  - Automation Services
  - Management Services
  - Seminar company

- Large corporation
  - Consolidated Plan
  - Sales Division
  - Staff function (2)

- Mfg. & Distribution Company
- Government Agency
- Non-Profit
- Church
- Association

As you review these plans, you will note that they all follow the One Page Methodology fairly closely... but not necessarily... precisely. That's OK! Each of these plans is a real plan, written by an executive, business owner or entrepreneur... so their personal style comes through!

Note: Sample plans have these consistent characteristics

- Vision Statements paint a graphical picture of what is being built.
- Mission Statements are short, most are 8 words or less.
- Objectives are always graphable!
- Strategies describe how the non-profit, department, project or program will be built.
- Action Plans describe the work to be done... all have completion dates.

The HR Consulting Group

Sally McKenzie & Bob Wilson

FY2018 Consolidated Plan

vision

Within the next 3 years grow The HR Consulting Group into a $1 million North Texas consulting and training company specializing in human resource training and consulting services for companies within a 50 mile radius of Dallas/Ft. Worth that have between 50 and 500 employees.

mission

Bring Preventative HR Programs to Growing Companies!

objectives

- Achieve 2018 sales of $350,000.
- Earn pre-tax profits of $75,000; after paying two partner salaries of $100,000.
- Consistently have partners bill out 6 days per month at $1,500 per day.
- Generate $40,000 from audits & assessments.
- Increase training program & product revenue from $7,500 a month to $10,000 by Aug. 30th.
- Increase ave. bi-weekly attendance at employer council meetings from 12 to 20 by May 15th.
- Produce six notable, publishable case studies this year.
- Take a minimum of 2 one-week vacations in the next twelve months.

strategies

- Become known for preventing catastrophic employee problems that destroy businesses.
- Attract clients with 50 to 500 employees, business owners who want preventive solutions.
- Promote initial trial through our monthly employer council meetings & low-cost guide books.
- Generate revenues thru preventive audits & assessments, training programs & consulting.
- Use technology/Internet for tele-classes, audits & assessments, & selling training guides.
- Strategically align our firm w/ local employment law attorneys, CPAs & business consultants.
- Continue to create books, guides, audiotapes, & assessment products from existing services.
- Build a business that is ultimately not dependent on my presence; which will make it sellable.

action plans

- Publish "Employer's Bill of Rights Handbook" by Feb. 28th.
- Complete Sexual Harassment, Family Leave & Diversity Guidebooks by April 20th.
- Launch "New Manager Training Series" May 1st; repeat program once in Q3 & Q4.
- Begin hosting monthly "Managers Problem Solving Roundtable" in July.
- Complete makeover of website & e-commerce systems by Sept. 30th.
- Introduce Smart System's web-employee appraisal process to our clients starting Nov. 1st.

Future Best Practices, Inc.

James McIntire, President

FY2018 Business Plan

ONE
PAGE
PLAN

---

vision

Within five years, become nationally known author, publisher, speaker and consultant serving entrepreneurs and independent business owners. Consult primarily in greater Boston metro area; approximately 30% of my time. Create products (books, tapes, CDs) for the entrepreneurial market 25% of my time. Speak extensively regionally, building to national recognition. By 2018 total revenues will be $500,000 or more.

---

mission

We help business owners build strong companies with best practices!

---

objectives

- Generate total revenues of $175,000 in FY2018.
- Achieve profit before tax of $90,000 in FY2018.
- Increase active consulting client base from 20 to 30; increase consulting fees to $90k.
- Secure 12 paid speaking engagements in FY18 at average fee of $2,500.
- Sell 1,000 books in FY18; 25m in FY19; 50m in FY20; 100m in FY21.
- Train 10 registered/certified E-Mgmt practitioners by 12/3/18; 100 by 12/31/19.
- Complete E-Mgmt audio tape by 8/31/18; sell 500 tapes yielding $5,000.
- Complete Profitability is No Accident book by 12/31/18 – sell 500 copies in FY19.

---

strategies

- Collaborate to complete; can't do this by myself… Always keep it simple!
- Use personal contacts to create opportunities to speak, get reviews, articles published.
- Self publish to start, prove marketability, seek national publisher.
- Create products & programs for others to sell that serve the entrepreneurial market.
- Seek endorsement/approval/intros; Quotes from noted authors, CEOs, SBA.
- Build national brand & corporate identity.
- Exit strategy; sell to major publisher or business training company in 5-7 years.

---

action plans

- Complete E-Mgmt. by April 2018; print 6,000 copies in May, 2019.
- Publish article in Inc. Magazine 4th quarter 2018 or 1st quarter 2019.
- Develop publicity & marketing plans by 3/31/2018.
- Develop E-Mgmt Certification program by 7/31/2018.
- Contract w/Audio Design Productions for audio tape production by 7/15.
- Submit articles to Inc., Entrepreneur, Home Base Business for December publication.
- Complete mailing to 250 trade associations by 8/15 for speaking engagements.

ZXM Automation Consulting, Inc.

Allen Marcus, President

FY2018 Consolidated Plan

vision

Within the next five years build ZXM Automation into the premier west coast industrial process automation consulting company specializing in integration solutions. ZXM Automation revenues will grow from $10 million in 2018 to $20 million by 2022 by expanding its role from a manufacturing representative company to a complete engineering field service and process solutions company.

mission

Helping you control your marketing, sales, service and distribution channels!

objectives

- Grow business 20% & achieve total sales revenues of $12 million in 2018.
- Achieve profit before tax of $1 million.
- Land at least 5 significant system projects at a minimum of $250k each in 2018.
- Increase gross margin from 17% to 20%.
- Increase sales per employee from $320,000 to $375,000.
- Increase Engineering Services billable utilization from 50% to 70%.

strategies

- Sell total solutions not parts.
- Significantly increase valued added engineering & integration service capabilities.
- Expand geographically into So. Calif., Oregon/Washington, Nevada, Arizona, Alaska.
- Aggressively target niche markets in each geographic market.
- Expand thru selective acquisitions and/or strategic partnerships.
- Continually develop the discipline of profitability for ZXM & our clients.
- Attract/retain key employees by maximizing their creative, technical & business talents.
- Share growth & prosperity w/ employees through incentive & equity participation

action plans

- Critical Marketing Program: Visit all 25 base system clients in 2nd Q.
- Hire System Eng. by 4/30 and Sales Mgr. by 6/30.
- Implement Client Awareness & F2K Support Programs in 3rd Q.
- Complete UC Berkeley, Lipton, SAI projects successfully by 9/30.
- Implement F2K Demo website in 4th Q.
- Install new NT server by 3/31 & Unix server in 2nd Q.
- Implement Sales Automation Program and complete conference room demo in 3rd Q.
- Complete business practices, procedures & policy manual by 12/31.

Jordan Business Seminars

Tom Jordan, Owner

FY2018 Business Plan Summary

ONE
PAGE
PLAN

---

vision

Within the next year, build a highly efficient marketing program to catapult our web graphics seminar business to $500,000 annual revenues.

---

mission

Help graphic artists migrate their businesses to the web!

---

objectives

- Sell 2000 Seminar seats nationally in the next 12 months yielding $408,000 in revenue.
- Sell an average of $46 per attendee books and tapes at each seminar; $92,000 in revenue.
- Earn a pre-tax profit of 25% or $125,000.
- Increase gross margin to 72% on seminar seats.
- Maintain COGS on books and tapes at 66%.

---

strategies

- Direct mail to purchasers of Adobe Products.
- Stress the business opportunity rather than the fact they will be learning software.
- Offer book and tape set bundles to increase average purchase.
- Increase the amount of on-site sales people to increase seminar sales.
- End quantity discounts on multiple sign-ups from single company.
- Utilize temp agencies in each seminar city to supply additional sales help.

---

action plans

- Redesign seminar mailer to stress business opportunity by January 15th.
- Design promotional piece to highlight better margin book and tape bundles by April 1st.
- Launch email newsletter to promote seminars by June 30th.
- Hire writer by March 3rd to edit new online newsletter.

Z-TEC, Inc. – Consolidated Plan

Jerome Johnson, CEO

FY2018 Plan

vision

Within the next three years build Z-TEC, Inc. into a $2 billion global provider of integrated workflow management solutions for Fortune 1000 companies, major municipalities and significant governmental agencies at the country, state, regional and federal level. Z-TEC, Inc. will be headquartered in San Francisco with offices in New York, Dallas, London, Singapore and Rio de Janeiro.

mission

Building Industrial Strength Business Systems!

objectives

- FY2018 Revenue of at least $900 Million.
- FY2018 Profit before Interest & Taxes of $85 Million.
- Complete at least 300 new installations and obtain 500 new clients by EOY 2018.
- Migrate at least 250 existing clients to Z-TEC web product cost reduction program.
- Increase Gross Margin from 51% to 55% through product cost reduction program.
- Increase sales per field employee from $250,000 to $300,000 in FY2018.
- Reduce Accounts Receivables from 60 days to 45 days.
- Achieve FTE head count of 1,500 by 9/31/18.

strategies

- Growth: Grow 50% each year by development of new clients and migration of existing clients.
- Reputation: Product position & strong reputation from existing client/partner referrals.
- Partnering: Align with industry leaders, partnering for marketing & solution development.
- Competitive Position: Optimize user/based pricing & modular system concepts for flexibility.
- Product Approach: Configure rather than Customize, Business Rules vs. custom programs.
- R&D: WorkFlow Solutions, Open Systems, multiple environments, Object-Oriented, flexible.
- Develop aligned team, know the plan, have sense of urgency, responsibility & accountability.
- Develop Employee Incentive Program to allow the team to share in the rewards & have fun.

action plans

- Implement Power Partner Initiatives w/Oracle UK by 3/31/18.
- Complete development of the Z-TEC client/server product by 3/31/18.
- Develop Sales & Marketing Resource Plan by 3rd Quarter 2018.
- Develop Partner strategies w/PeopleSoft, Sun Micro, IBM by 4/30/18.
- Launch Europe Customer Forum in London at June 2018 Convention.
- Develop Sales Force Automation Plan by August, implement in 4th Quarter 2018.
- Implement financial reporting system at project/dept. level by Oct. 2018.
- Implement professional skills development program by Nov. 2018.

Z-TEC Inc. – Southern European Sales Division

Alex Morgan, Sales Division Mgr.

FY2018 Plan

vision

Within the next three years grow the southern Europe division of Z-TEC into a $150 million business unit with offices in Madrid, Barcelona, Nice and Florence.

mission

Find customers… close contracts!

objectives

- Increase sales to $45 million in FY2018.
- Complete installation of 50 systems in FY2018.
- Increase gross margins from 51 to 55% by increasing sale of value added services.
- Increase contribution margin to $20 million.
- Migrate at least 35 existing clients to Z-TEC internet product by 12/31.
- Reduce accounts receivable from 60 to 45 days.
- Achieve FTE head count of 275 by 9/31.

strategies

- Partners: Align with industry leaders, partnering for marketing & solution development.
- Product Approach: Configure rather than customize business rules vs. custom programs.
- Market Positioning; modular systems for flexibility, customization; premium pricing.
- R&D: Workflow solutions, open systems, multi-platform, object-oriented, flexible.
- Develop an aligned team with sense of urgency, responsibility and accountability.
- Develop employee incentive programs to allow the team to share rewards.

action plans

- Implement Power Partner Initiatives w/Oracle Spain by 7/31.
- Launch European Customer Forum in Spain at June convention.
- Develop Sales Force Automation Plan by 08/31/18, implement in 4th quarter.
- Implement financial reporting system at project/dept level by 10/2018.
- Implement professional skills development program by 11/2018.
- Complete Portugal facilities upgrades by 10/31/18.
- Build communication and team performance among 12 branch managers.

Z-TEC, Inc. – Controller

Gail French, Controller, European Division

FY2018 Controller's Department Plan

vision

Within the next five years, build an integrated accounting function at Z-TEC that provides complete accounting support services, management & business analysis and budgeting & forecasting to properly support Z-TEC at $2 billion in revenue.

mission

Provide tools & information to manage growth… profitably!

objectives

- Increase gross margins from 38% to 45%.
- Identify and implement $150k in cost saving projects.
- Close and issue monthly financial statements by the 15th of each month by September 30th.
- Reduce Z-TEC accounts receivable from 65 days to 55 days outstanding.
- Pay off line of credit by September 30th..

strategies

- Build a Z-TEC financial services team that can grow with Z-TEC by training/empowerment.
- Build a business mentality by providing training on fin. statements, budgets & forecasting.
- Increase gross profit by creating mgmt. reporting on non-billable time and material.
- Control expense by dept. budgets, use of policy, forecasting system, timely financials.
- Streamline acctg. process w/ operations dept. to minimize month end billing bottlenecks.
- Improve cash flow thru weekly AR collection monitoring and reduce billing errors.
- Streamline the payroll and HR process thru remote data entry and integrated systems.
- Eliminate duplicate data entry/manual reporting by consolidating to one operating system.
- Finance growth thru internal funds and bank debt; control expense/keep margins high.

action plans

- Build initial Financial Reportings, IS, BS, Dept. expense, sales repts. by February 28th.
- Streamline monthly closing procedure by February 28th.
- Train staff in new closing procedure by March 31st; complete job descriptions by April 30th.
- Build Banking System direct deposit to lockbox by Feb 28th.
- Build 2019 budget analysis model by August 31st; finalized by September 30th.
- Investigate new payroll system w/HR systems by October 31st.
- Finished 2019 budget by Dec 15th.

Z-TEC Inc. – Personnel Manager

Jonee Grassi, Personnel Manager

FY2018 Plan

vision

Develop a world class workforce of employees for Z-TEC International and their independent contractors who fuel the growth of the company through their creativity, dedication, and capabilities.

mission

Attract, build and retain a world-class team.

objectives

- Recruit 1,600 new employees by EOY; end year with 3,600 employees.
- Decrease turnover rate from 18% to less than 10%.
- Decrease overtime from 22% to 10% by April 15th.
- Increase average learning program hours/employee to 60 per year.
- Achieve internal promotion rate of 60%.
- Increase flex-scheduling optimization to 90% by September 30th.

strategies

- Hire world-class team players with exceptional skill sets whenever possible.
- Retain our employees by treating them as strategic partners critical to our success.
- Commit to have resources, people & systems in place before they are needed.
- Ensure career development through innovative training & development programs.
- Highly compensate employees for their contribution; generous use of stock options.
- Support work-life balance through flex scheduling and well-being programs.
- Develop Employee Incentive Programs to allow our team to share in the rewards.

action plans

- Implement Z-TEC Employee Hiring Campaign by 01/15/18.
- Launch Employee Distance Learning Program by 02/01/18.
- Develop Intranet Flexible Scheduling facility by 04/2018; implement by Q3 2018.
- Complete national salary survey by 06/31/18.
- Upgrade Kansas City national training facilities by 06/2018.
- Implement professional skills development program by 11/2018.

Colorado Garden Window Company

Mike Bozman, CEO

FY2018 Consolidated Plan

vision

Within the next 3 years grow Colorado Garden Window Company into a $40 million national home products company specializing in manufacturing and distributing custom and replacement garden windows and skylights to baby-boomers and home remodelers.

mission

Bring Light, Air, and the Beauty of Nature into homes… through creative windows!

objectives

- Achieve 2018 sales of $17 million.
- Earn pre-tax profits in 2018 of $1.5 million.
- Target Cost of Goods Sold at 38% of sales.
- Reduce inventory levels to 3.3 months on hand by August 31st.
- Grow Garden Window Division at 8% per year & achieve $5.3M this year.
- Expand skylight/custom window product lines; grow sales to $7.5 million this year.
- Implement profit improvement programs & reduce product costs to 38%.
- Achieve 98% on time delivery with 98% order accuracy by 1st quarter.

strategies

- Focus on new upscale home developments and baby-boomer remodeling trends.
- Build Colorado Garden Window Co. into a nationally recognized brand name.
- Control quality processes by manufacturing solely in-house.
- Become vendor-of-choice by maintaining a constant inventory of standard window sizes.
- Increase capacity & manufacturing efficiency by actively reducing duplicate products.
- Centralize distribution into one location; reducing costs & improving service.

action plans

- Introduce new scenic Garden Window at S.F. products show 3/15/18.
- Roll out new package design beginning 3/31/18.
- Expand Sales Dept. to focus on Signature Homes in Denver and Provo by 4/1/18.
- Introduce inventory reduction program company-wide by 5/1/18.
- Fully implement new MRP software to achieve inventory reduction by 7/1/18.
- Complete skylight product rationalization program by 8/15/18.
- Research, design and roll out re-designed employee benefit program by 10/1/18.
- Complete product distribution consolidation project by 11/15/18.

Meals on Wheels

Donna Van Sant, Executive Director

FY2018 Business Plan Summary

ONE
PAGE
PLAN

---

vision

Grow Meals On Wheels program into a premier nutrition service for the home bound elderly and disabled adults in our county, providing a full compliment of quality prepared meals and personal attention seven days a week.

---

mission

At home and healthy with full nutrition and personal attention.

---

objectives

- Provide services to 475 home bound elderly each month.
- Provide expanded nutritional service products to 300 individuals.
- Add new customers at the rate of 45 per month by May 1.
- Increase case management revenue to an average of $2,500 per month.
- Recruit and train 25 new route drivers, both volunteer and paid by July 15.
- Obtain $80,000 in county contract and foundation funding by September 30.
- Provide 12 in-service training sessions for route drivers and 24 for MoW staff.
- Provide nutrition services to 75 disabled adults each month.

---

strategies

- Develop and maintain effective relations with funders; program tours, and proposal writing.
- In conjunction with food services vendors, develop three new products for our customers.
- Develop and execute a customer focused marketing plan for nutrition and CS management.
- Create and execute a staff and volunteer development plan that works!
- Operate our customer feedback and quality control system to increase customer satisfaction.

---

action plans

- Complete new product development by March 23rd.
- Complete staff hiring and support plan by May 16th.
- Hold program tour and meeting with all current funders by October 10th.
- Win funding from 10 new foundations by November 23rd.
- Develop a marketing plan by December 1st.

---

vision

Within the next three years achieve a fire and emergency services team in the City of Pageville that is characterized by high employee morale and excellent community service.

mission

Elevate citizen confidence that their fire and emergency services are dependable and affordable. Protecting community with quality life… and fire-safety services.

objectives

- Reduce fire response time to 5 minutes average by 12/31.
- Reduce freeway emergency response time to 7 minutes average by 12/31.
- Reduce loss of property by 12% from previous year.
- Assure there is no more than a 5% deviation from last year's monthly overtime budget.
- Reduce worker injuries to no more than 6 per month by 12/31.
- 60% employees involved in participation activities by 7/01.

strategies

- Involve community in neighborhood targeted life and safety program.
- Involve all personnel in every aspect of life and fire safety at their locations.
- Establish and enforce performance based accountability system at all department levels.
- Establish and provide professional growth and opportunity programs for all personnel.
- Coordinate with other agencies to meet emergency response standards.
- Deliver safety education & other services within our mission to the community.
- Aggressively work to prevent hazardous conditions.
- Respond promptly to rescues, fires, medical emergencies and natural disasters.
- Ensure safe, professional, environmentally harmonious actions.

action plans

- Develop a coordinating mechanism to keep track of all elements of the strategic plan by 3/31.
- Accountability systems are developed for all elements of the strategic plan by 6/1.
- Implementation of the strategic plan is monitored on a monthly basis by 7/31.
- Develop a list of comparable cities and fire departments to benchmark our services by 9/1.
- A commitment plan to guide building of a policy maker consensus on service levels by 10/1.
- Implement a comprehensive employee involvement plan by 10/31.
- Implement a comprehensive community involvement plan by 12/31.

Unity of Marin, Spiritual Center

Reverend Richard Mantei

FY2018 Consolidated Plan

ONE
PAGE
PLAN

---

vision

The vision of Unity In Marin is to provide a loving and supportive diverse community which teaches practical Christianity and encourages spiritual growth and action. Within 3 years 700 will attend 3 transformational Sunday services, and a mid-week, and monthly healing service. We will have an active 7-day per week spiritual center and have 100+ children in YE with 40 personal growth and spiritual education class night/events for adults per mo. UIM will have 3 effective outreach programs in Marin County and beyond. People will experience a deep sense of spiritual community, personal transformative growth and service to others as a path to God.

---

mission

Discover divinity within and reach out in loving service.

---

objectives

- Increase Sunday attendance from 220 to 400 by July 1.
- Increase annual income from $380,000 to $620,000.
- Increase Y.E. weekly attendance from 15 average to 40 average by March 1.
- Increase new membership from 75 to 100, increase AE class 12 to 25 attend 160 to 450.
- Increase Spring and Fall in-home program from 100/150 to 180/220.
- Increase Service Ministry involvement from 105 to 150.

---

strategies

- Bld upon successful Sunday Celebration: enhance music & pre/post service experience.
- Meet goals of FIA/CC/LegacyEndow/other profit making events thru excellent in execution.
- Bld Edu. success by increased variety/continuity & excel in curric & teachers.
- Deepen prayer consciousness by expanding role of chaplains, outreach and education.
- Bld membership by better marketing & outreach prog.& congreg. involve.
- Bld upon MLT success by inviting/recognizing/ coaching/thanking excellence in leadership.
- Leverage minister's time by evolving staff and leadership teams.

---

action plans

- In Q1 Complete negotiations & details for 6 nat'l speakers to appear during 2017 by 1/31.
- In Q1 Complete Sunday, seminar, theme programming for the year by 3/15.
- In Q1 Complete arrangements for once per month healing service.
- In Q2 Finalize plans for a mid-week service to begin in September.
- In Q3 Have 75% of work done in preparation for a 2019 Capital Campaign to launch 4/2019.
- In Q4 Fully implement transition team for YE leadership by 10/31.
- In Q4 By November 30th, complete plans to implement 2019 Capital Campaign 4/201.

Bay Area Entrepreneur Association

George Cole, Executive Director

FY2018 Strategic Plan

vision

Build BAEA into a nationally recognized micro-enterprise organization with an extensive greater San Francisco Bay Area network of entrepreneurial support groups providing nationally recognized products, programs and services to entrepreneurs, small business owners, and partner organizations.

mission

Create viable businesses and successful entrepreneurial leaders through networking, support and connection to resources.

objectives

- Increase membership from 150 to 300 by 12/31/18.
- Launch 2 networks by 6/2018 and add 3 more networks by 6/2019.
- Generate $8,000 from entrepreneurial programs, events and products in FY 2018.
- Host 3 regional network events with at least 50 attendees each and generate $3,000.
- Conduct 4 workshops/programs with an average of 25 participants and generate $4,000.
- Increase low-income members to 25 and increase minority members 25% by 3/2018.
- Award 5 scholarships totaling $1,300 in FY 2018.
- Recognize 10 entrepreneurs for outstanding business growth & community service.

strategies

- Use public relations and media to share successes, educate, recruit and fund.
- Market and sell BAEA endorsed products and services nationally.
- Collaborate with nat'l micro-enterprise org. in nat'l awareness programs and funding.
- Establish BAEA center to create long-term community presence & financial asset base.
- Enlist key community leaders and businesses to launch and develop new networks.
- Attract/retain low-income entrepreneurs by offering scholarships funded by corp. sponsors.
- Utilize multi-lingual/cultural programs to attract minority entrepreneurs.
- Package successful BAEA programs & products to sell to other micro-enterprise orgs.
- Use technology to manage growth, streamline ops., and deliver programs, & sell products.

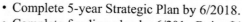

action plans

- Complete 5-year Strategic Plan by 6/2018.
- Complete funding plan by 6/201. Raise $100,000 by 11/2018.
- Hire executive director by 11/2018.
- Expand board of directors from 4 to 7 by 11/2018.
- Develop BAEA product and service marketing plan by 8/2018.
- Develop 2-year network expansion plan by 6/2018.
- Launch sales/marketing plan of One Page Business Plan by 6/2018.
- Collect and write 20 success stories by 7/2018; Implement PR Plan by 8/2018.

Notes

Final Thought...

Most of us have no shortage of good ideas! The issue is which ideas are we going to act on?

Learn how to say no to "good ideas"... yours, your partners, employees, associates, friends and family. You only have time, money and resources to execute against the "great ideas." The great ideas can be written on the back of an envelope. They are memorable! They catalyze people and businesses.

Planning doesn't need to be complex! Keep it simple!

Jim Horan
President
The One Page Business Plan Company

Here's What Entrepreneurs, Business Owners and Executives are Saying about their One Page Plans

"Putting together a 70-page business plan – replete with charts and graphs and spreadsheets – is a walk in the park. Getting it all right – exactly right – on a single page. Whoa! "Beautiful systems" are simple. One page business plan = the proverbial better mouse trap!"
Tom Peters
Best-Selling Business Author, Manchester Center, Vermont

"Using Point, Click, Plan! I had a solid draft of my plan within a couple of hours! After reviewing it with my team, they wrote plans w/ Point, Click, Plan! In a couple of days the entire team had solid plans ready for review and alignment. This is the new way to plan! No wasted time. Time previous spent on planning is now being spent on execution. We have procedures in place to revisit the plans quarterly, and we look forward to putting together next year's plan even quicker!"
America OnLine
Craig Peddie, Vice President and General Manager, Seattle, Washington

"We have found the web-based One Page Planning and Performance System valuable in managing our core business over the past two years. It provides a useful structure for our quarterly review meetings that helps us better focus on those things that make a real difference in our company!"
The Ken Blanchard Companies
Tom McKee, CEO, San Diego, California

"The One Page Planning method, along with the web-based tool, are great ways to help our managers stay strategic even though their days may be spent working primarily on tactical issues."
Herman Miller (San Francisco Franchise)
PJ Anderson, CEO, San Francisco, California

This is an innovative, fresh approach to business planning. If all loan applicants would provide us with clear, concise summaries of their business plan, a banker's life would be a lot easier.
Bank of Walnut Creek
Jim Ryan, Chairman and CEO, Walnut Creek, California

"We have used The One Page Business Plan with great success in the last two years! This web-based system will revolutionize and streamline our planning and performance management processes and improve our bottom-line results! The skills learned in writing a One Page Business Plan have helped bring a disciplined focus to our business.
Drake Beam Morin
Ken Kneisel, Executive Vice President, Atlanta, Georgia

"It's very easy for stockbrokers to get wrapped up in the market and lose perspective. In order to be successful for the long run, one must have a plan and The One Page Business Plan is a great tool."
Morgan Stanley Dean Witter
Ralph Miljanich, Vice President, Santa Cruz, California

"The One Page Business Plan is the business owner's Cliff Notes."
DaMert Company
Fred DaMert, Chairman, CEO & Chief Toy Maker, Berkeley, California

Want a New and Profitable Reason to Call on Current and Former Clients?

As a licensee, you will:
- Add significant consulting revenues to your firm.
- Produce significant results for your clients... quickly!
- Add value to your firm with our global brand.
- Have a powerful prospecting tool with a high conversion rate.
- Have access to state-of-the-art web software that is only available through our licensees.

Your clients will also enjoy a number of other benefits including:
- Users spend less time planning and more time implementing.
- Plans are more effective because every user has a plan that is integrated with the total plan.
- Communication is stronger between departments due to system's open-book capabilities.
- Stronger accountability with web-based Scorecards & Progress Reports.
- With a short learning curve, focus is on performance & implementation, not learning software!

We help you Sell More Consulting!

We help support your sales efforts, from a fully functioning web-based demonstration site to professional sales materials and hands-on system training sessions. You'll also benefit from our national branding efforts that include a best-selling business planning book. Best of all, you will participate in an ongoing Advanced Practice Development Program designed to grow your entire business!

You Can Make Money with The One Page Business Plan:

Our powerful tools can create spectacular breakthroughs in sales and profitability for your firm. Here are four of our popular offerings... serving four different market segments!

$50,000 One Year Performance Management Program

$5,000 One Day Owner or Executive Planning Retreats

$3,000 Executive/Business Owner Plan Development

$750 Small Business QuickStart Program

Additional information about our certification programs is on the Consultant's Toolkit CD and at our website: www.onepagebusinessplan.com